Stock Trading

Strategies to Make Money with Stock Trading

Warren Richmond

© **Copyright 2017 by Warren Richmond - All rights reserved.**

The contents of this book may not be reproduced, duplicated or transmitted without direct written permission from the author.

Under no circumstances will any legal responsibility or blame be held against the publisher for any reparation, damages, or monetary loss due to the information herein, either directly or indirectly.

Legal Notice:
This book is copyright protected. This is only for personal use. You cannot amend, distribute, sell, use, quote or paraphrase any part or the content within this book without the consent of the author.

Disclaimer Notice:
Please note the information contained within this document is for educational and entertainment purposes only. Every attempt has been made to provide accurate, up to date and reliable complete information. No warranties of any kind are expressed or implied. Readers acknowledge that the author is not engaging in the rendering of legal, financial, medical or professional advice. The

content of this book has been derived from various sources. Please consult a licensed professional before attempting any techniques outlined in this book.

By reading this document, the reader agrees that under no circumstances are is the author responsible for any losses, direct or indirect, which are incurred as a result of the use of information contained in this document, including, but not limited to, —errors, omissions, or inaccuracies.

Table of Contents

Introduction

Chapter 1: Getting Started with Stock Trading Strategies

Chapter 2: Setting up a Strategic Plan

Chapter 3: Profit from a Falling Stock

Chapter 4: Day Trading

Chapter 5: Position Trading

Chapter 6: Reversal Trading

Chapter 7: Swing Trading

Chapter 8: Fundamental Analysis

Chapter 9: Technical Analysis

Bonus Chapter: Penny Stocks: Risks and Rewards

Conclusion

About the Author

Introduction

In the previous book of the series, Beginners Guide to Stock Trading, you learned about the basic fundamentals of the process that constitutes stock trading. In this book, we go a step up and focus on the strategic part of trading. Even though the first book gave you a reasonably good idea about what stock trading entails, we all know that Rome wasn't built in a day, and you will need to understand the process in a lot more detail than was possible to explain in the first book.

This is especially true with regards to the fact that stock trading is more of a well-planned and executed methodology of making money than it is a casino-like environment where on a good day, you can make the fortune of a lifetime. As a matter of fact, this is precisely the reason why so many people who should be investing in the stock market and taking advantage of its ability to provide stellar returns are reluctant to do so. This is a real pity because stock trading has the ability to transform people's lives like nothing else can.

The prospect of *gambling away* their hard earned money on the stock exchange scares them off. While it is true that investing in the stock market carries an element of risk, the way to deal with it is to gain a deep and insightful understanding of how the market operates rather than steering clear of it. There is risk in crossing the road and flying as well, but that does not stop us from doing those things.

The thing about stock trading is that if you don't misconstrue and misunderstand it, it can almost be viewed in a spiritual right. The potential of unlimited wealth creation that stock trading carries can transform the lives of millions and make people's wildest dreams come true. That, in and of itself, probably propels millions to try their hand at stock trading.

Then again, it is money made by honest means by studying the market and industry conditions very carefully. So it is money made from the sweat of one's brow just as it is in the case of any other kind of earnings from your profession.

The economy of the world keeps on growing. Earlier, it was the US and Europe that were the engines of growth. Now there are newer regions including India, China, Asia, the Pacific region and so on. NASDAQ and FTSE and not the only indices to track; there are so many more.

Opportunities abound and along with them so does complexity.

But all the same, getting intimidated is not the answer and the way to stay relevant is to change with the times and adopt new technology. As a matter of fact, more and more people from around the world are taking to stock trading than ever before. The stock markets of the world are very democratic institutions these days and allow anyone and everyone to trade with a click of a mouse.

In fact, there is a silent revolution underway that is allowing millions around the world to increase their wealth by trading.

If this were not the case, there would not be so many people from different walks of life who have been perfectly able to make a great deal of money by trading on the stock market. This book will show you exactly how. As with the last book, this new addition will carry a summary of every chapter at the end, along with actionable steps you can take to hone your trading skills.

"Frankly, I don't see markets; I see risks, rewards, and money." – *Larry Hite*

Chapter 1: Getting Started with Stock Trading Strategies

1.1 - What is a Stock Trading Strategy?

Let us not begin our initiation into stock trading strategy by using some heavy jargon, as there will be enough of that later in the book. In a simple and straightforward language, any well thought out plan that helps an investor obtain profitable returns over the short or long term can be termed as a stock trading strategy. You could also refer to it as a disciplined and structured way of buying and selling stocks taking care to adhere to certain set guidelines when taking strategic trading decisions. So, as I mentioned before, there is nothing ad-hoc about it.

The stock market and stock exchanges are an integral part of popular culture around the world and that is testimony to the power of stock trading and what a hold it has on popular imagination. This is something that has been the case for centuries now and it is likely to remain this way-probably forever.

Common Stock Trading Strategies

There are a number of time tested and effective stock trading strategies that form the bedrock of any serious endeavor of making money on the stock exchanges and savvy stock traders use them quite effectively. Some of these are described below:

- **Day Trading:** As you might have guessed by the name, this type of trading entails buying and selling securities within the space of a day. As this kind of trading requires close monitoring of the prices of the securities being traded through the day, it was usually the professional and full time traders who indulged in it, but the advent of online trading has seen all manner of people from different walks of life taking to it. Today, most people know what day trading is, or at least they think they do. It has acquired very glamorous undertones though there is actually nothing glamorous about it.

-**Scalping:** This is an innovative trading strategy which involves carrying out a very large number of trades on the same day, often in the hundreds, with the hope of making a little profit on each trade, by virtue of taking advantage of the bid-ask spread (the difference between the maximum price a buyer will pay and the lowest price at which a seller is ready to sell).

This works best when the trader buys at the bid price and sells at the ask price in order to capitalize on the price difference. You need to be psychologically primed to be able to handle this, as there is a lot of tracking involved.

-*Swing Trading*: In times of price volatility, when many traders would bide their time until the prices settle down, the swing traders come into their own, hoping to gain by buying and selling smartly in these conditions. Typically swing trading lasts for about two days but may extend as much as fifteen days.

Swing traders usually try and follow some trading guidelines that are derived from a study of market fundamentals that are often algorithm based. Again you need to be able to hold your nerve in this kind of trading.

-*Position Trading*: A position trader formulates a short to medium term trading strategy by analyzing short term to long term trading charts. Depending upon the kind of trend they thus analyze, position traders may carry out their business over a few days, a few weeks or even longer.

They are a little bit like surfers in that they will try and ride any wave they notice in the market and usually end

Do you see yourself in any of these categories? Possibly more than one? Good, for you are getting a hang of the stock trading business.

Stock Trading Strategies Viewed in a Historical Context

You have all heard about the Merchant of Venice. There is a reason that Shakespeare based his epic play in that city. The moneylenders of that great Italian city stepped into areas that the major European banks would not look at. They would trade debts amongst themselves. For instance, somebody might want to exchange their risky but high-interest loan for a safer but low-interest loan with another lender, they were there to facilitate it. Not just that, they evolved to a stage where they started buying government debt issues and even started selling debt issues to individual customers.

The first stock exchange of the world was born in 1531, in Antwerp, Belgium, though the instruments traded were principally bonds and promissory notes. The several European East India Companies which were floated with the express purpose of financing risky sea voyages to the East, in the hope of profiting from the sale of the merchandise if the ships made it safely home, were an integral part of the story of the rise of the stock exchanges. In order to spread out their risks, these companies would invest in several ships simultaneously.

These were the first instances of limited liability companies that functioned like modern companies in that they issued stocks and paid dividends out of the profits made by all the voyages sponsored by the companies. This led to an increase in the value of the shares held by the company and they began to grow in size and make more and more profits for the investor.

Part of the reason for the success of these companies was that they were backed by Royal Charter that forbade competition. The shares of these companies were issued on paper and could be sold to other investors. The government backed British East India Company was particularly successful and buying a share of joint stock companies became the flavor of the times.

This led to lots of businesses, particularly the South Seas Company, issuing shares of their companies to an eager pubic ever ready to buy them. As was to be expected in the absence of a proper revenue model, these companies could not pay dividends and crashed. Greed and avarice existed then, as indeed it exists now! This led to the banning of the issuing of shares for many years in England. Mankind never really fundamentally changes. Just the technology does.

The New York Stock Exchange was founded in 1792, nineteen years after the London Stock Exchange. It quickly became central to all business and trade that occurred in the United States. As the US economy grew to its preeminent stage, the NYSE established itself as the primary stock exchange of the world.

The New York Stock Exchange quickly became a symbol of world capitalism as much as the hammer and sickle of communist Russia became a symbol of world communism. Along the way, the symbol of communism got consigned to the dustbin of history and capitalism triumphed.

While the NYSE clearly dominated the world economic stage right through the 20th century, the road into the 21st century may not necessarily be the same one. Of course, the tremendous advancements in communication technology have meant that major financial centers like New York, London and Tokyo now straddle the global marketplace. However, in so far as deciding one's personal investment portfolio is concerned, it would make sense to stay clued in abreast of whatever trends emerge in the years ahead, rather than extrapolating past occurrences in helping you plan for this.

In a sense, the evolution of the stock exchanges and stock trading has marked the evolution of mankind itself since the advent of the modern times. Like us, stock trading has changed shape and nature many times and with each newer version, it became better and better and more accessible. The modern Internet era has transformed it the most and now, with the advent of algorithms and artificial intelligence, one really does not know the final shape that it will assume.

1.2 - Stock Trading Strategies are Critical for Becoming a Successful Stock Trader

While it is all very well to aspire to be a stock trader, one would do well to remember that one cannot do so in a vacuum. You have to have a well thrashed out stock trading strategy in place or you are setting yourself up for failure. Well begun is half done they say and this is certainly true when it comes to trading.

It is important that one understand that stock trading has to be guided by a certain set of time tested guidelines that have been followed by all kinds of traders across different scales of operation. The individual guidelines by themselves are quite helpful, but if used in tandem with each other, greatly increase the chances of the stock trader making money.

The stock trader could be likened to a navigator who is trying to guide his or her spaceship in very daunting circumstances, where they have to dodge asteroids and meteors at every step even while keeping ship on course for its destination.

Benefits of Following a Stock Trading Strategy

- Your chances of success increase because you use proven methodologies.
- You will have factored in common mistakes that people have made in the past and not repeat those.
- Because of an increased chance of earning profits due to following a stock trading strategy, you will be confident in scaling up.
- If you are experienced in stock trading strategy will you consider the deployment of modern tools like software and artificial "intelligence."
- A well thought out stock trading strategy can help you make a fortune.

As everyone is aware, the stock market is a place where a fortune can be made in double quick time. Unless you are incredibly lucky, a well thought out and executed strategy is the only way that you can do that. The irony is everybody enters, or almost everybody enters, the stock exchange with the intention of becoming super rich, but don't take the right steps to get anywhere close to that stage.

Those who always use a well thought out strategy in their stock trading decisions are likely to become more and more efficient with time, leading to them making bigger and bigger profits with the passage of time, and that is what is essentially required.

Following is a stock trading strategy as described above that makes stock trading a less risky and more mainstream way of generating wealth.

Common Mistakes

While it is great to have a strategy and also identify the kind of trader you are, there are certain mistakes you should try to avoid.

-*No Plan*: There is an old saying that goes, 'if

you do not know where you are going, any road will lead you there'. It is always good to have a plan in mind. You need to ensure that you have your goals and objectives laid out in the plan.

-*Financial Analysis*: You have to analyze your finances in advance when you choose to trade in stocks. You have to remember that not every day is a good day and therefore you must plan your finances in case of a sudden unexpected loss.

-*Overconfidence in the Managers*: You may have asked someone to help you with trading in stocks. However, it is never good to place complete trust on them – you should question them and their methods often to understand if they have made the right decisions with your money.

-*No diversification*: It is always good to spread your finances across different stocks to ensure that you do not pool all the risk into one stock. This is to avoid a situation where you may lose all the money you own since you invested in only one stock.

-*Too short a time horizon*: Most investors always choose to invest only for the short term. It is always good to invest in a stock that you are certain will do well in the long run – say, 15 or 20 years. For instance, if you were investing in stocks to save up money for your daughter's college education, it would be best to invest when you are around 35 or 40 instead of waiting till you hit 50 which is closer to the retirement age.

1.3 Example of a Typical Stock Trading Strategy

Let us take an example of a Day Trading Strategy that may be followed by a new entrant. This will give you some handy lessons, as day trading is something that is catching on, on account of electronic trading having come into vogue:

Arm yourself with knowledge- You should be well versed not only in all aspects of the trading process, but also all the latest facts and information about events and happenings that might impact the price of stock. Additionally, it would be a good idea to be on the ball about stocks that one would like to trade.

Allocate a Budget- You have got to be sure about how much money you are willing to risk on each trade that you embark upon. The amount that you so allocate should not be more than you are willing to lose.

That is not to say that that is what will happen, but it makes sense to proceed with caution in day trading, as you don't want to over extend yourself.

Apportion Time-While day trading may be a great way to make money quickly, it is not going to happen if you don't allocate most of the day to the activity. You have got to be keeping track of the opportunity and speed is of the essence.

Begin Small- Day trading requires great focus on the stocks that you are trading and it makes sense that you start small. A stock or two a trading session is the maximum you should be looking at.

Trade at the Right Time-Until the time you become quite conversant with the finer nuances of day trading, it makes sense to avoid the first fifteen minutes of the morning trading session, when volatility is at its peak. The hours in the middle of the trading session, though quieter, offer the appropriate time period for a newbie to pick the right cues.

CHAPTER SUMMARY:

In this first chapter of the book, you have learned about the essential elements of a stock trading strategy as well as getting an idea about the most common stock trading strategies that people follow. You also got to know the historical context in which stock trading began and evolved internationally over the centuries.

It was explained to you why it is absolutely essential to formulate an effective stock trading strategy. The guidelines provided by such a strategy would enable you to substantially enhance your chances of effectively leveraging the power of stock trading to make money. The chapter also explained to you the precise benefits of following an effective stock trading strategy.

Lastly, you were provided with the example of a typical stock trading strategy (day trading), which a new entrant to stock trading may follow.

Your Quick Start Action Step

You have now moved from knowing the basics of stock trading to getting to understand the nuances and nitty gritty of stock trading. At this stage, you are advised to arm yourself with as much knowledge about the finer aspects of stock trading.

It might be a good idea to do some reading on the website shown below-

http://www.moneycrashers.com/best-stock-market-investment-news-analysis-research-sites/

An investment pays the best interest in knowledge-*Benjamin Franklin*

Chapter 2:

Setting up a Strategic Plan

2.1 Significance of Strategic Planning for Stock Traders

Anybody who wishes to be a professional stock trader needs to understand that, as they are in effect embarking upon a business, they have to have a plan or strategy in place to take their business forward. Just like in the case of any business plan, a stock trading business plan too will have to evolve with time and continue to propel you on the path of growth.

If you do not have a strategic plan to take your stock trading business forward, you are hardly likely to witness success. It may require you to make an effort to learn the various kinds of strategy required to get a handle on the stock market and its vagaries but, with time and persistence, you should be able to reach success and learn how to profit from trading on the stock market.

Stock traders need to educate themselves about strategic planning, as it is the only thing that will safeguard them against the high rate of failure in this business. While there is no doubt about the fact that trading can make you extremely rich in a very short period of time, the fact of the matter is that this rarely comes about as a fluke, and is more often than not the result of an intimate knowledge of the market and the ability to devise the right strategy to leverage it.

A stock trader who does not follow a strategic plan is akin to a pilot who flies without a flight plan. You wouldn't want to be in that plane, would you? Then how can you think of trading without the help of a strategic plan? After all, disasters don't always occur in mid-air.

Day Trading Sans Plan Leads to Failure

Only about 10% of those who indulge in day trade find success. Why is that? The answer is the lack of a sound strategic plan. Take the case of a day trader who, by an extraordinary streak of luck, has managed 9 consecutive successful trades. Know that each trade carried with it a $100 profit possibility and a $50 risk. The 9 successful trades handed this person a neat $900 profit. The 10th trade went badly, as one might expect and this person suffered a $50 loss.

Instead of not pushing his or her luck and quitting, this person bought additional shares at the lower price hoping to reduce his cost of buying. The person continued to lose money until he or she reached their last hundred dollars, which left them in a quandary about whether to sell or hold.

This is what happens when you don't plan your stock trading approach. Here was a person who had a 90% success rate, but still ended up in a bad shape because he or she had no idea about how to manage risk.

The number of disastrous trades made by someone who had made a fortune prior to that, is legion. As you surely don't want to join their ranks, you should have a plan in place.

2.2 Strategic Plan Comes Before Stock Trading Strategy

Stock trading is essentially an exercise in wealth creation. Before you begin to create a well thought out stock trading strategy, and hit the deck running, it might be a good idea to have a clear idea about why you plan to get into stock trading in the first place.

This is where your strategic plan comes in. You have got to have a goal or vision behind your decision to get into stock trading. For instance, you might want it to be your full time profession. Another reason behind your decision could be to deploy your surplus money constructively. Yet another objective might be to make a certain amount of money in a certain period of time.

Once you are sure about why it is that you are going to be a stock trader, you can get down to the business of formulating the best strategy to help you achieve your objective or objectives. It is always good to know why you are going to be at war before actually commencing the shooting!

Advantages of a Plan Preceding a Stock Trading Strategy

You will be able to come up with a better stock trading strategy that is aligned with the plan. It brings focus to your stock trading strategy and you are less likely to lose focus and deviate from your core strategic objectives. You will be less inclined to follow a high-risk strategy if it is dictated by an overall strategic plan or objective. It provides you with the right reason to be stock trading in the first place. Even the best of stock trading strategies cannot exist in a vacuum. It has to have an end objective in place. A stock trading strategy that is not tied to a larger objective is little better than aimless gambling.

2.3 - Why Creating A Strategic Plan Leading To A Stock Trading Strategy Is Important

Ensuring that there is a clear rationale behind why you need to trade - You have to have an absolutely clear idea about why you want to get into stock trading, before you a move a step further in that direction. Once you have that part clear, your plan becomes your compass or even your conscience keeper.

Identifying What Motivates You - You have to know why you want to trade - perhaps to create an additional revenue stream or to invest your surplus money. For some it might be their desire to get rich quickly. It may even be on account of funding your children's educations. Whatever might be your motivation, being clear about it provides you a perspective about the path ahead.

What Are Your Skills - Before you commit yourself to creating a stock trading strategy, you have to know how well you are equipped to undertake stock trading. How much capital do you plan to commit and are you aware of the nitty gritty of the trading process? Do you come from a business background or do you hold a job?

All of these factors are going to have a crucial impact upon your ability to formulate an effective stock trading strategy.

Risk Taking Ability - Any business entails some risk, but these are higher in the case of stock trading and it is not a good idea to get into it if you are fundamentally averse to taking risks.

Identifying The Challenges- It might be a great idea to conduct a SWOT (Strengths, Weaknesses, Opportunities, Threats) analysis about your decision to get into stock trading so that you don't encounter any nasty surprises later.

Forewarned, as they say, is forearmed and only if you are sure that you can handle the rough with the smooth should you go ahead and start working out a stock trading strategy.

CHAPTER SUMMARY:

In this chapter you found out how critically important it was for anyone thinking of getting into stock trading to have a clear strategic plan about what they plan to achieve by doing that.

Considering the high rate of failure in stock trading, the absence of a clear strategic vision about one's reasons for trading will, more likely than not, lead to failure. Only if you know your reason for wanting to get into stock trading, should you take the next step of formulating a strategy.

You learned why it is imperative to have a strategic plan thrashed out before you get down to the business of devising a cutting edge stock trading strategy. You were also made conversant with the specific advantages of adopting this approach.

You got to know why it was so important that the strategic plan has to lead to the stock trading strategy. This is because it lets you know exactly how well placed you are to not just survive, but thrive, in the rough and tumble of stock trading.

(Write here, in numbered order, a summary of the past 3 sub-paragraphs that is a recap of the chapter.)

YOUR QUICK START ACTION STEP:

You are now well into thick of things and it will do you a world of good if you spent some time every day reading the financial papers, watching business news and surfing the Internet to find informative articles about stock trading strategies.

You may find reading this article quite useful-

https://www.forbes.com/sites/johntobey/2015/09/14/what-investment-strategy-is-best-in-this-stock-market/#4ab93eda53c9

"I will tell you how to become rich. Close the doors. Be fearful when others are greedy. Be greedy when others are fearful." - Warren Buffett

Chapter 3:
Profit from a Falling Stock

What Does Selling Short Mean?

Now we are in this for real! Short selling describes the process under which someone sells a stock that they either do not own or have borrowed. This is done with the expectation that the stock's price will decline, enabling the seller to buy it back at a lower price, resulting in a profit.

There is a huge inherent risk in selling short as one's expectation of the share price falling may not turn out to be true and one may end up buying the shares at a higher price than at what one sold them and make a loss. The buying back of the stock is inevitable because it needs to be eventually returned to the owner.

Short selling is really not everybody's cup of tea because of the great risk of incurring a loss and is generally resorted to by people who have a wealth of experience behind them in such matters.

Difference between Selling Short and Selling Long

If you can sell short, it stands to reason that you can sell long. Of course, selling long is nothing like selling short. For one thing, you have to actually buy the stock rather than borrow it, and you do so with the expectation that the price will rise rather than fall.

Profiting From a Falling Stock

Most people imagine that the sun only shines on the stock markets when the prices are rising and popular culture seems to support this contention. However, the fact of the matter is that the savvy stock trader makes money even in a falling market.

In any case, experts reckon that most long term investors will see their stock value decline from peak valuation to about half of that at least once if not twice or thrice in their lifetime.

Great Instance of Making a Killing from a Falling Stock

In the summer of 2015, a the stock of a US rail company, Kansas City Southern, that was underperforming in the market was expected to continue to drop for some time. With the shares falling to $99.23 one expected an 8% drop for the shares to $91. Instead of going for a short option, as might be expected, it was suggested that one might try a put option.

This is something that gives the investor an option to sell the stock at a specified price (strike price) on a future expiration date. This arrests the risk associated with a stock with a falling price.

What was recommended here was that investors buy $105 striking puts slated to expire in December at $10.30 a share. That would cost the investor only $1030 as each option contract pertained to 100 shares. This came out way cheaper than shorting 100 shares at a 50% margin, which would have cost $4961. As things turned out, the KSU stock fell much faster than expected, getting to the target of $91 in only 17 days leading to an annualized return of a mind boggling 771.3%!

- Selling Short To Gain Profits

Of all the strategies worth considering in one's pursuit of gaining profit from stock trading, selling short is certainly worth considering and a most intriguing one, especially for those who are new to the business.

Now that you know what short selling is, you also know that you don't really need to be a financial wizard to dabble in it, but you certainly need to have a fair bit of stock trading exposure and an understanding of the dynamics of the market to be able to use short selling as an effective profit making strategy. There are a number of benefits that come your way when you short sell. Given below are the principal ones:

Short selling lets you make a profit even in a falling or bearish market.
As stocks fall way faster than they rise, you make profits that much faster. You might make a higher profit in a month of short selling than you might make in a year of holding a long position. It provides flexibility to your investment plan in that you can make profits both when stock prices are rising and when they are falling. To take a farming analogy you can sow a crop in both summer and winter!

- Steps Constituting a Short Sale

- Hypothetical company ABC trades at $50 per share on March 1
- The trader enters a market short sell order for 100 shares at that price.
- The stock value diminishes by $10 to $40 per share.
- The trader makes a profit of $1000(minus commission and other charges) at the rate of $10 per share multiplied by 100 shares

CHAPTER SUMMARY:

In this chapter, you learned what one means by selling short, as also the difference between selling short and selling long. That apart, you learned how to profit from a falling stock. Other than that, you read about a real life instance of profiting from a falling stock. You were taught the exact process of selling short to gain profits. Lastly, you were taken through the steps of the process that constitutes selling short.

YOUR QUICK START ACTION STEP:

You are now in the thick of things. Learn some more about selling short by visiting this link:

http://www.investopedia.com/university/shortselling/

"The stock market is filled with individuals who know the price of everything, but the value of nothing." - Phillip Fisher

Chapter 4:
Day Trading

4.1 What Is Day Trading?

For all the hype surrounding day trading, it is pretty straightforward process that involves buying and selling of shares over the period of a single day with the express intention of making a profit, arising out of the fluctuation in share price.

In the past day, trading was the sole preserve of financial services companies because only they possessed the wherewithal to carry out such trade. The advent of electronic trading, however, anybody can carry out a day trade if that is what it is that they want to do.

Historical Basis behind Day Trading

In so far as stock trading goes, day trading, as we recognize it in modern times, is of pretty recent vintage. The genesis of day trading is tied up with the arrival of electricity. Day trading has its early beginnings in 1867, when the introduction of the telegraph made it possible for stock markets to create the first ticker tape that made it possible to relay information about transactions occurring on the exchange floor to brokers.

In those days, individuals did not have direct access to the market and all trading had to happen through brokers. You can imagine that carrying out day trading in such circumstances would not have been easy at all.

Things progressed quite a bit when, in 1971, the National Association of Security Dealers (NASD) created an electronic communication network, which was given the name National Association of Securities Dealers Automated Quotation System, which we now know as NASDAQ. This, for the first time, made day trading more accessible and convenient for the common man.

Another big step forward in making day trading more broad based was the abolition of fixed commission and making trading fee an outcome of market conditions. This reduced the cost of trading for the individual trader and consequently day trading received another fillip.

The small traders received further protection in the aftermath of the 1987 stock market crash when the Small Order Entry System (SOES) was introduced. Under this system, orders of 1000 shares or less were to be given a priority over larger order by the brokers to prevent them from shortchanging small customers while taking orders to execute a trade on the phone.

The Dot Com era in the late nineties saw individual investors take to day trading in a big way with profit margins on day trades routinely going as high as 400%. Still, this was early days in terms of volumes when compared with today's figures.

On the whole day, trading didn't really have a very wholesome reputation in that period and people generally mistrusted it. The fact that 70% of day traders lost everything they had invested didn't do much to shore up the confidence of the people. As a matter of fact, there are still those who consider day trading nothing short of gambling. Of course, there are also those who consider any kind of stock trading repugnant. Talk about throwing out the baby along with the bath water!

Another thing that negated the advantage of day trading was the repealing of SOES in 2000. Furthermore, the bursting of the dot com bubble made a large number day traders bankrupt. Henceforth day trading became pretty much like any other kind of stock trading with both professional and occasional investors resorting to it when required. Your skill as an overall stock trader determines how well you can leverage day trading.

Today at a time of job losses and news of artificial intelligence and robots taking away the jobs of millions, day trading looks more attractive than ever before. If one were to only do it with the same measure of seriousness that one looks at a regular job, one may have a great career on one's hands. What's more, with the way things are these days, what with the progress and technology the bots may lend you a helping hand in this.

4.2 - Day Trading - A Great Short Term Strategy for Stock Trading

If you want to be a successful stock trader, whether on a part time basis or as a full time professional, you would do well to understand that day trading can be a great short term strategy that can help you get ahead.

What you have got to understand about day trading is the fact that it is all about timing the market. The very essence of this strategy is to time your purchases and sales in a fashion that lets you buy low and sell high.

Now, if you can do this with a fair bit of accuracy by relying on a detailed study and analysis of the market conditions, the companies whose shares are listed and the factors that have a bearing on share prices, you will have devised a great short term strategy for making a fair amount of money by stock trading.

The fact is that whoever is looking at using day trading as an important component of their overall stock trading strategy, has to understand that day trading requires your time. You have to be involved in it through the trading session or there is very little likelihood of your making a success of it.

You have to be under no illusions that day trading is a short cut for getting very rich quickly. If that were the case, everybody would do it. On a contrary day, trading is very difficult and requires relentless focus and hard work to succeed.

So if you thought that day trading was like winning a lottery, you have another think coming. It is not. It is a very serious business and requires all of your thinking prowess to succeed. For you to be successful, your level of commitment has to be extraordinary. So if you see the gambling kind take up day trading and even succeeding in a trade or two, don't pay them any heed and approach day trading in the right professional way.

Benefits of Day Trading

- **Be Your Own Boss** - If you happen to be a professional day trader you have complete independence and autonomy. You will report to no one, nor be answerable to anyone. You will be an entrepreneur in the truest sense, living by the fruits of your decisions.
- **Financial Independence** - You don't have to depend upon your job, or worry about managing a business if you are a successful day trader. You will have full financial independence.
- **Great Highs** - The high from making a neat profit or even a small fortune in the space of a day is unmatched and unparalleled. That you achieve it entirely on you own adds to the sense of euphoria.
- **Reputation** - There is something of an aura associated with day traders and, in a sense, they almost have a mythical reputation among many. If you want to be part of that, then day trading awaits!

4.3 - Day Trading-Steps to Execution

- **Know if it is for you** - Successful day trading demands total dedication and adequate knowledge with regards to finance, market conditions and mathematical analysis, and so on. If you think you have it in you, go right ahead.
- **Organize the capital** - Know that you will not always have profitable trades. So it is important to have the cushion of adequate capital. For professionals, one might look at a sum of about $100,000 to trade with though beginners and amateurs may well look at smaller sums.

- **Know the market** - You cannot not know the market in an in-depth manner and hope to do well. Everything from trading hours and the days that the exchanges are closed due to holidays to knowledge about margin requirements, the influence brought to bear on the stock market by news and so on.

- **Putting an appropriate trading strategy in place** - You cannot operate in a vacuum. It would make sense to get to understand one or two approaches that you might want to start with.

- As time goes on, and you become better at it, you can have a number of sophisticated short, medium and long term strategies to help you get ahead.

- **Strategy Should Be Part Of A Larger Plan -** Your strategy necessarily has to be part of a larger plan. It has to move according to parameters like timing of entry or exit, the amount of capital required, the frequency of trading and so on.

- **Simulate Before You Start -** These days, brokers offer you a test account, which allows you simulate a real life trade with virtual money. Try your hand at this and check out how good you are and once you are confident of your abilities, move on to real trading.

CHAPTER SUMMARY:

This chapter focused on day trading beginning with explaining what day trading was all about and then going on to explain how it evolved historically. You learned why day trading is a great short-term stock trading strategy. That apart you got to understand the benefits that accrue from day trading.

The steps that help you start day trading were explained to you

YOUR QUICK START ACTION STEP:

As mentioned earlier you might want to hone your skills at day trading by trying a simulated version. That apart, you might want to read about it on https://www.thebalance.com/day-trading-4074032

"In investing, what is comfortable is rarely profitable." - Robert Arnott

Chapter 5:
Position Trading

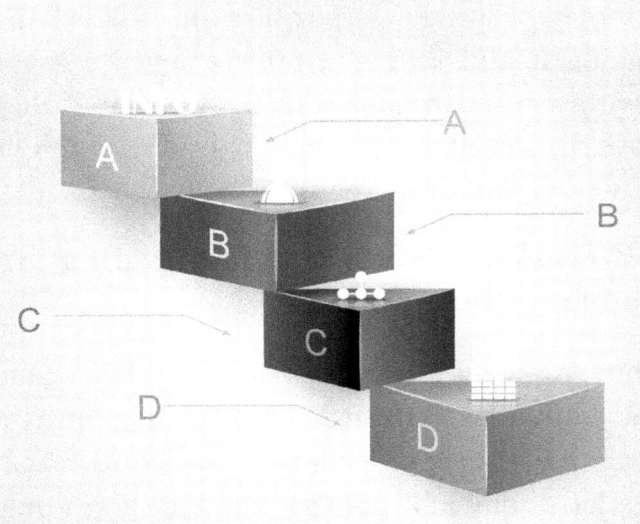

5.1 What is position trading?

A position trader is a person who holds a position for a time period that extends into weeks or months. They do not concern themselves with minor price fluctuations but instead focus on a major trend.

So they will take a position on a stock by buying it and selling it after a few weeks or months in accordance with the trend that they have discerned. So, unlike day trading, there is no close monitoring required.

Difference between Position Trading and Long Term Buying

Though position trading has a long term time frame that extends from weeks to month to years it differs from long term investing in that the latter buy and hold for the long term only with the view of profiting from a rising market by way of only long trades.

A position trader though not concerned about short-term price fluctuations, but does refer to weekly and monthly price charts to evaluate the market and may deploy both long term and short term trading strategies to make money.

An Instance of Position Trading

In any position trade, three parameters rule - a planned entry, a predetermined exit and managed risk. Take the case of XYZ stock, which you may plan to buy when the price goes beyond a 40-week moving average. On placing the trade, care is taken in using a stop loss in case the share price starts falling. This is kept at 5% below the moving average.

In the initial period, the market is quite choppy and does not develop leading to losses. A few months down the line, the price once again crosses the 40-week moving average, which is a signal to buy. As this price is $16.61 the stop loss at 5% is placed at $15.78.

The exit isn't planned until there is a weekly close below the 40 days moving average. This happens in about three years when the weekly close price is $46.57 and the opening price the following week is $46.76.

5.2 - Position Trading a Great Strategy for Beginners and Professional Traders

For both beginners and professionals, the biggest allure of position trading lies in the fact that it does not require a great deal of involvement of their time. After one has carried out the necessary initial research and analysis, all that one needs do is place one's trade and not carry out any detailed monitoring, as one has to do in day trading. You may want to check on the stock on a weekly or monthly basis, but that is about all as a position trader is not concerned about minor price fluctuations.

This makes for tension free trading which can only augur well for stock traders, both beginners and professional. Position trading lets the stock trader milk the trends to the maximum, as they do not have to regularly trade and thereby lose on account of spreads. Even the chances of making mistakes over longer trade period are considerably lower giving the stock traders considerable leverage.

Benefits of Position Trading

- No impact of short-term stock price fluctuations.
- Relatively stress-free trading on account of less amount of monitoring required.
- Getting the maximum return from a trend.
- Less chance of errors as the trader is over a long period of time, which

provides more leverage.

5.3 Basic Steps of Position Trading

Determine the size of your risk - It doesn't matter how much money you are investing -a few thousands, tens of thousands or hundreds of thousands - never put more than 1⅜ of your capital on a single trade.

Get a handle on the trade risk - To make position trading safe, you have to have a stop loss level. You really need to figure out the trade risk level to determine what the right-positioning size in dollars is.

Find out the positioning size - Once you are aware of your trading budget and the risk factors, you can decide on what the size of your position will be. Of course, your position size will vary from trade to trade as the factors impacting it will have changed as well.

Arrive at a proper position trading strategy - With time and experience, you will be in a great position to determine your position size by studying the signals emanating from trade.

CHAPTER SUMMARY:

In this chapter, we learned all about position trading. In particular, we learned how to distinguish it from long-term investment.

> We also learned of an instance of position trading.

We learned how position trading is a great stock trading strategy for both beginners and professionals.

> We learned of the benefits of position trading.

We learned of the basic steps behind position trading.

YOUR QUICK START ACTION STEP:

You must be finding the book quite interesting, considering how far we have come. Here is something else you might want to read:

http://www.dummies.com/personal-finance/investing/technical-analysis/how-to-adjust-trade-positions/

"How many millionaires do you know

who have become wealthy by investing in savings accounts? I rest my case." - Robert G. Allen

Chapter 6:
Reversal Trading

6.1 What Is Reversal Trading

Any stock trader who takes the trouble of studying the technical charts pertaining to a stock's price can obtain a fairly good idea of when a reversal will occur. For instance, if a stock's price has been consistently breaching higher and higher levels or plummeting to lower and lower depths, traders would be right in imagining that a reversal is around the corner. While reversals are very common in day trading, these are also witnessed over many days or weeks of trading.

The tendency of stocks that show marked gains or losses to reverse over a short term frame is often used as part of a strategy to make gains on highly liquid stocks, usually in a time frame of about a month. Trading reversals are undoubtedly one of the most stimulating yet risky trading strategies.

There can, of course, be many reasons for reversals. It may be on account of a number of reasons, but usually, supply and demand is the basic one. When there are more buyers than sellers, the price goes up and vice versa. Factors such as a change in interest rate or a new government policy too can impact this demand and supply.

An Instance of Reversal Trading

Take the case of K. Kellogg Company tracked over a 12-month period from July 2013 to June 2014. From July to February, the trend was generally falling with the low point coming in February after which there was a share price rally that took it beyond the former high point in January.

There was a higher move up in March that was barely stopped by a pull back. With both the high and low getting higher, an uptrend indicated a reversal had been created.

6.2 - Learning Reversal Trading Is Important For Stock Traders

Both new traders, as well as the dyed in the wool ones, will do well to learn reversal trading as that can help them make fewer losses and have a larger number of winning trades to their credit.

However, the rub of the matter lies in the fact that reversals are very difficult to pinpoint. But if one can learn how, it is quite an effective strategy for making money. What works out in favor of the trader who uses a reversal trading strategy is the fact that the entry levels are quite low.

Advantages of Reversal Trading

- It allows better entry points that allow one to buy low and sell high.
- Greater chances of making profits.
- Lower losses
- A larger number of winning trades to the stock traders' credit.

6.3 - Steps to Reversal Trading

- Identifying a higher time frame level.
- Reading the higher time frame reversal signal.
- Perfecting the lower time frame entry timing.
- Learning when to stay in the trade and when to exit.

CHAPTER SUMMARY:

You learned what reversal trading is all about. You also learned about an instance of reversal trading.

You learned why learning reversal trading is good for all stock traders and what the advantages of reversal trading are.

You learned of the important steps of reversal trading.

YOUR QUICK START ACTION STEP:

You are now reasonably well versed with reversal trading. You may now want to do up some reading about it.

You can start with this:

https://www.warriortrading.com/reversal-trading-strategy/

Chapter 7: Swing Trading

7.1 - What Is Swing Trading?

Swing trading is essentially a short term trading method of trading stocks. Swing trading may be done over two to six days to up to two weeks.

The idea behind swing trades is to identify the main trend and then endeavor to make a profit by carrying out swing trading within that trend.

Difference between Swing Trading and Long Term Investing

The principal difference between these two types of trading is pertaining to time. In swing trading, one holds the stock from one day to many days in the hope that one will benefit from the price swings. Long term investing, on the other hand, entails buying stock and forgetting about it for years on end - for any length of time (5, 10, 20 years; even a lifetime).

As swing trades are of a shorter duration, these tend to be more intense and require greater monitoring on your part. Long term trades don't require you to do much after investing for many years, except hoping that you will make a profit.

An Example of Swing Trading

This example pertains to Electronic Arts (ERTS). Here is how it went. The market happened to be overbought on June 15th so there was a huge possibility of the market falling, which made it the right time for selling short. At the end of the day, the trader found that the stock had rallied and consolidated at a given point.

Then the trader analyzed the hourly charts and saw the area where the consolidation happened and planned to put his stop above that. The trader did not see the price rising above this resistance level. Now was the time for exiting with a profit.

7.2 - Learning Swing Trading a Must for Any Stock Trader

Swing trading is great to know for both amateur and professional stock traders. It combines the convenience of day trading with the added advantage that it gives you more time to study and take your trading decisions. You neither have to spend all your time in front of the computer terminal, like in the case of day trading, nor do you have to be committed for long periods of time. The thing about swing trading is that the gaps created by overnight trading can act both in favor of and against the trader.

Advantages of Swing Trading

- **Focus** - Since the time frame is generally short, you can focus on core market movements and quickly discern a trend.
- **Quick Results** - With swing trading not lasting more than a month, one gets to learn from the success or otherwise of the strategy pretty quickly.
- **Saves Time** - As swing trading does not require very detailed and close monitoring, you get to save a lot of time.
- **Less Risk** - Swing trading has smaller stop losses than those of long trades. This makes it inherently less risky.

7.3 - Steps to Swing Trading

Reading the charts to discern a trend
Identifying the appropriate entries and exits by understanding the support and resistance levels on the chart.
Keeping the risk manageable by ensuring the right positioning sizing.

CHAPTER SUMMARY:

You learned what swing trading is and how it is different from long term investing. You also learned of the difference between swing trading and day trading. That apart, you learned about a real swing trading example.

You learned why swing trading is great to know for both amateur and professional investors. You learned of the advantages of swing trading as well.
You learned of the steps to swing trading.

YOUR QUICK START ACTION STEP:

As you learn more and more trading nuances you need to read up more about what you have read. How about this- http://www.investors.com/ibd-university/swing-trading/

It's not how much money you make, but how much money you keep, how hard it works for you, and how many generations you keep it for." – Robert Kiyosaki

Chapter 8: Fundamental Analysis

8.1 - What Is Fundamental Analysis

You will hear these words bandied about a lot in trading circles. What does it mean? When you carry out the fundamental analysis of a stock you are, in a sense, trying to find out what its true or real value is by studying economical, financial and other critical data associated with it.

By identifying the true value of the stock in question and juxtaposing it with its current value, one will come to know whether it is overvalued, undervalued or rightly valued. This will help you take a considered decision regarding the stocks to be traded.

No stock trader worth his while would enter the stock market without arming themselves with the essential knowledge that comes their way by carrying out a fundamental analysis. If you ever try being with serious stock traders and this is all that you will hear them talk about. The same is the case with all the business news channels.

While earlier you would have been fazed by much of the jargon they would use, with the reading of this book, you will understand almost everything they say, if not everything. This is the thing about stock trading. There is a whole universe out of there. The more you become a part of it, the more you understand the processes involved, the better your grasp of the nuances of stock trading and the surer that you will be of your trading abilities.

As a matter of fact, something like fundamental analysis does not come easily. You have to have been doing it for a very long time to actually start getting good at it.

When you do the fundamental analysis, you are doing stuff that is normally carried out by economists, MBAs and corporate head honchos. Will you still imagine that there is nothing to stock trading?

Not only is all this knowledge handy in trading, but can also be used in other walks of life. To that extent, stock trading does cause you to brush up your skills in more ways than one and these can be put to use in myriad ways.

You have got to be able to understand economics, science, commerce, accounts, and statistics. That is quite a lot of stuff that you have to learn.

The great thing about trading is that it makes you carry out a lot of research about industries, companies, government policies as well as brush up your mathematical skills. Whoever said that stock trading is for dummies has another think coming.

Fundamental Analysis Is a Good Short Term Trading Strategy

Short term investing is infinitely riskier than long term and it is therefore important that one makes the right call. This is where fundamental analysis comes to the rescue. You need to be able to watch and understand how the average price of a stock behaves across a time frame.

Then you have to be able to understand how the market cycles across the months behave. You have to learn the science of managing risks by using sell stops and buy stops at the right moments in time. Above all, you have to be able to use technical analysis that leverages knowledge gained from past behavior of the stocks and market and use it to try and predict future behavior. Then there are buy and sell indicators, indices, and patterns that need to be considered.

Elements of Fundamental Analysis-

In the previous paragraph, we got to know about some of the elements of fundamental analysis. An important one though wasn't mentioned and that is a company balance sheet, the studying of which tells you more about the health of a company that you may be tracking than anything else.

A balance sheet lets you know exactly how much does a company have by way of both assets and liabilities. The difference between the two lets you arrive at the equity value of the company.

8.2 - Why learning Fundamental Analysis As a Strategy Helps Traders

All kinds of stock traders - long, short, day and long term - could do well to make fundamental analysis a vital part of their trading strategy. The reason is that any strategy minus fundamental analysis of the stocks you are going to be putting money on is no strategy at all.

You have to have some technical basis for your investment. It can neither be a leap of faith nor left to chance. The thing is that fundamental analysis will work most of the time, even though you can't predict when it will fail.

That is hardly any reason for not using it. All the same fundamental analysis will work better for long time investors because there is more data to examine for a longer period of time.

Benefits of Fundamental Analysis

- Helps with long term investments by its critical inputs. You will now be more sanguine about committing money for longer periods of time.
- Helps identify companies with good value. This aids in picking the right stocks.
- Helps you understand the business and industry pertaining to the stocks that you trade, inside out. This again helps you take the right call on your trades.

Once you have spent the right amount of time perfecting fundamental analysis and start getting your predictions right, you will be in an enviable position, and people will seek you out for your advice. That should really be the endeavor of any serious stock trader- to be that perceptive.

That actually is the very essence of trading. Without fundamental analysis to guide you, you will be like a rudderless ship adrift in the ocean on a foggy night.

8.3 - Steps to Using Fundamental Analysis

- Analyze economic factors that include the prevailing state of the economy, and

specifically the industry the relevant stocks pertain to.
- Analyze company specific factors pertaining to a company's financial statements, management strengths and growth outlook.

Making sense of the data. This will help traders zero in on the stocks to be picked.

CHAPTER SUMMARY:

You learned what fundamental analysis is and why it makes for a good short term trading strategy.

You also learned about the elements that constitute fundamental analysis.

You learned why learning about fundamental analysis benefits all traders. Besides, you learned about the direct benefits accruing from fundamental analysis.

You learned the steps to fundamental analysis.

YOUR QUICK START ACTION STEP:

Things are really heating up now and you now know so much more about the whole business of stock trading. All the same, it might be a good idea to do some reading about the subject.

Check this out-

https://zerodha.com/varsity/module/fundamental-analysis/

***Financial peace isn't the acquisition of stuff. It's learning to live on less than you make, so you can give money back and have money to invest. You can't win until you do this.** - Dave Ramsey*

Chapter 9: Technical Analysis

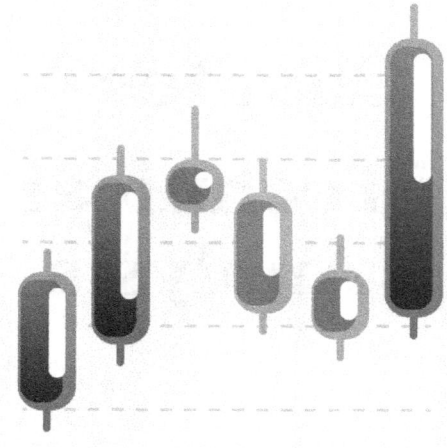

9.1 - What Is Technical Analysis?

Technical analysis enables traders of stocks to technically analyze shares by studying data pertaining to trade activities with the express intention of predicting the future movement of stocks. This is done by analyzing past price movement and volume.

Technical Analysis as a Good Short Term Strategy

Technical analysis is really tailor made for short term strategy. This is because technical analysts are typically very active traders who hold short positions so as to take advantage of the fluctuating price of stocks.

Whenever a technical analyst type of trader encounters a resistance level, it will be his or her cue to enter into a short position.

While fundamental analysis theorizes, technical analysis tells it as it is. One understands by studying technical research charts that the market does not always follow cold logic. At times it flies in the face of it.

The thing about technical analysis is that, unlike fundamental analysis, technical analysis has fewer assumptions and more fact. This is a report from the trenches if the former is a report from the headquarters.

Constituents of Technical Analysis

As you are aware, technical analysis of stocks requires the studying of a lot of data pertaining to past performance of the stock. Line charts, for instance, are the most basic form of data, which show price changes over a certain period of time.

A bar chart, on the other hand, displays the open, close, low and high prices of stocks. This is done by way of a series of bars, which represent the price movement of stocks over a certain period of time.

9.2 - Why Learning Technical Analysis Helps All Stock Traders

At any time, trading is fraught with risk and any mechanism that shines a light on what needs to be done in order to maximize profit and minimize loss is welcome. The analysis of past share price patterns and stock behavior can be effectively extrapolated to obtain a fair idea of the path ahead for all manner of stock traders including novices and accomplished ones.

One cannot possibly only depend upon fundamental analysis for taking the right call on investment. Equally, if not more technical analysis, needs to be carried out to understand the nuances of trading.

Advantages of Technical Analysis for Traders

It has become quite easy to use these days, what with software enabling one to quickly study and interpret charts enabling one to trade with greater confidence.

There is no need to spend time analyzing detailed financial statements of companies being tracked.

Instead of going strictly by facts and figures of fundamental analysis, technical analysis lets the trader feel the actual pulse of the market.

9.3 - Steps to Using Technical Analysis

- **Keep it simple -** Don't use too many indicators. Use the popular ones like Moving Average (MA), Exponential Moving Average (EMA) and so on.
- **Test the indicators with historical data -** Do as much testing you can and see what works best for you and then trade. The more you test, the better your skills will be in actual trades.
- **Have a proper stop loss in place -** Always do this, as it does not make sense

to hold a losing stock for way too long. Stock trading cannot be reduced to a zero sum game. You have got to know when to advance and when to retreat.

There is an old saying that says that the soldier who flees the nettle-field lives to fight another day.

Know when to sell - Your technical indicators can fail you and the patterns cannot guide you in the right direction sometimes. That is the cue to sell even though your instinct tells you that it is a good thing to continue a winning trade. As a matter of fact, in trading sometimes when all logic fails, it is considered wise to not disrupt any good run of fortune. Nevertheless it has always got to be a call taken on the spot at the right time.

CHAPTER SUMMARY:

You learned about technical analysis and how it is a good short term trading strategy. You also learned about the constituents of technical analysis.

You learned how learning technical analysis can help all stock traders. Besides, you learned about the advantages that accrue from learning technical analysis.

You learned of the steps that help you use technical analysis.

YOUR QUICK START ACTION STEP:

By now you should be reasonably well steeped in the dynamics of stock trading. Reading some more about it can only help enhance your knowledge. Check out this link-

http://www.investopedia.com/university/technical/

Investing should be more like watching paint dry or watching grass grow. If you want excitement, take $800 and go to Las Vegas." - *Paul Samuelson*

BONUS Chapter
Penny Stocks: Risks and Rewards

10.1 What Are Penny Stocks

Penny Stocks are largely those stocks that trade on the major stock exchanges at extremely low prices, which of course leads to very low market cap (market capitalization). As a rule, these stocks are extremely speculative and extremely risky on account of their low liquidity, poor following and disclosure norms.

Having said that, I would like to reiterate the fact that it remains a very risky investment proposition that is not everybody's cup of tea. However, for those who understand what Penny Stocks are and are not averse to taking risks, this offers very good value because of their low price. So even if you have a small budget you can look at making a quick buck by investing in penny stocks.

But then Penny Stocks, despite being an outlier, are a mainstream form of investing that people do resort to. Knowledge they say dispels ignorance and if anyone harbors any such notions reading this chapter will remove them.

You might hear people react with horror if you mention that you are going to be buying penny stocks - almost as if the devil has invited you to a meeting. You can understand their disquiet though many people are not very sanguine about trading as such and trying to trade some lowly low priced shares that are not even market regulated or sold through some regular stock exchanges should look more than a wee bit fishy.

Investing In Penny Stocks as a Short Term Strategy

You might imagine that not many people would want to invest in Penny Stocks given their highly risky nature. But, on the other hand, a lot of people invest in these as a short term strategy attracted by low prices of the stocks concerned, which lets them buy a large number of shares. They view it as a good short term strategy of making quick money. It is not as if chances of making money come by that easily and if Penny Stocks can provide it, then why not go for penny stocks.

Though Penny Stocks have received a bad press and the term Penny Stock is a bit disconcerting, there is money to be made on them if you play your cards right. I may have used the analogy of cards, but you do need to approach Penny Stocks in a well-planned fashion

As long as you don't invest very large sums of money in them, invest in no more than a couple of stocks at a time, and exit on time (in the short run), you should be okay. So there you are. Penny Stocks are not bad after all. You may even consider buying them. The thing is, as long as you don't throw caution to the winds and do some basic checks, you might still leverage penny stocks quite well.

Beware the "Pump and Dump" Schemes

Another very off color term, a "Pump and Dump" scheme, is actually a scam and totally illegal. This involves the investors promoting a stock like there is no tomorrow and once this drives up the price, they go ahead and sell their holding at a profit. Now, this is the kind of stuff that gives Penny Stocks a bad name and unfortunately, it is quite commonly reported.

What one can be certain about human beings is that as long as there are loopholes they will try and exploit these and "Pump and Dump" stocks are a manifestation of this.

Such a stock is unscrupulously promoted as something that is expected to perform extraordinarily well, with the aim of pushing up the price. The idea here is to shift the demand and supply. This kind of vicious

Example of Pump and Dump Scheme

In 2014, a Connecticut money manager,

Abraxas J. Discala, CEO of OmniView Capital a privately held investment advisory firm. He was accused of manipulating the price of four microcap stocks, Code Smart, Cubed, Star Stream Entertainment and The Staffing Group.

The law enforcement authorities moved in anticipation of Discala dumping the shares of Cubed after driving up the prices.

10.2 Fundamental Analysis As Applied To Penny Stock Trading

One would imagine that something like Penny Stock investing would be the last thing to carry out a fundamental analysis for, but come to think of it, it really should be the very first. You have got to make some sense out of whatever little information that is available to you. But with things like "Pump and Dump" scandals being reported every now and then one can never be too careful.

A fundamental analysis may lead you to pick the right penny stock to invest in. It is because you are playing a high-risk game by investing in penny stocks and you had better get your facts about these right to minimize the risk.

But if you are able to play all your cards right and so end up making all the right trades you could end up one happy man thanks to you your interest in Penny Stocks. As Sean Connery said in one of his iconic reprisals of the role of the British Secret Service Agent, "Never say never again!"

All the same, considering that one cannot for sure trust the data being analyzed in the case of Penny Stocks the trader would be advised to use their personal discretion in making any investment decisions

Benefits of Investing In Penny Stocks

- **Low Price -** With the price of a Penny Stock at $5 and below it affords an investment opportunity to those with limited budgets. Also even if you ended with a loss it won't amount to much as the per-share cost is low.
- **Growth Potential -** Owing to their low price, penny stocks have scope for growth. So they might end up making you a fair amount of money.
- **Makes Your Portfolio Diverse -** A penny stock diversifies your portfolio in the short run while increasing liquidity.

10.3 Steps to Using Penny Stocks as a Trader Investor Strategy

See if it is right for you-This is a highly

risky form of investment as 95% of Penny Stocks are not worth the trouble. Get into it if you are serious about it.

Have goals- As with any other kind of investment, you have to have clearly defined goals with regards to your penny stock investments. Just because these stocks are of a nondescript origin, it does not follow that your strategy should be nondescript as well.

See if you are getting the right investment advice-If you are, you should be making money and it would make sense to stick with the source. No point in you trying another source. In any case, there won't be that many penny stock specialists, so you might as well as nurture the one good source that you have.

Target Specific Industries-So what if you are investing in penny stocks, you have still got to follow some method. So go ahead and become industry specific in your investment.

Choose Specific Companies Within The Targeted Industry Group-This is the next logical thing to do. At the end of the day, you do have to invest in individual stocks.

Liaise with the Investor Relations Person in the Targeted Company - Since there is so little information available for you to go by, liaise with the IR person in the targeted company as your go to person. More than any analyst the IR person will be in the know of the company's future prospects if any.

CHAPTER SUMMARY:

In this last bonus chapter of the book, you learned about Penny Stocks. You also understood why it was an effective shot term trading strategy to trade with Penny Stocks.
> You were also made wary of Pump and Dump schemes and actually provided with a real life example of that.

We also explained to you how fundamental analysis can be applied to Penny Stock trading. You were also apprised of the benefits accruing from this.
You were told of the steps to take to effectively use Penny Stocks as a trader investor strategy.

YOUR QUICK START ACTION STEP:

Well, we have come to the end of the book with this chapter on Penny Stocks. It was important that you be acquainted with all aspects of the stock trading process and this is exactly what has been achieved here. Keep reading about stock trading to keep yourself abreast with the latest development.

For now, you might want to visit this link and do some reading-

https://www.warriortrading.com/penny-stocks/

You get recessions; you have stock market declines. If you don't understand that's going to happen, then you're not ready, you won't do well in the markets." - *Peter Lynch*

Conclusion

Thank you again for owning this book!

I hope this book was able to help you to give you a pretty comprehensive idea of what stock trading is all about. This second book of the series has exposed you, dear reader, to stock trading in considerable detail and though it may take some time for all the lessons to sink in, it might be a good idea to refer to it again and again, until the time it all becomes familiar to you.

To all those who would have told you that stock trading is a path that not everyone can tread upon will not really be telling you the full truth. The fact of the matter is that, over the long run, there is no other form of investment that can deliver the kind of returns that stocks can.

Then there is the financial freedom that stock trading can provide you with. It can transform your dreary 9 to 5 lifestyle into something wonderful and magical. But to make all of that happen, you need knowledge - all that you can get. This book should only be the foundation upon which you will make a super grand edifice of success.

You have got to take a call about stock trading. Are you going to be only interested in it or are you going to dedicate yourself to it? That will be the difference between a winner and a loser. Once you are fully committed, you will have no choice but to make it work, come hell or high water.

This is how all the great success stories of trading came about. There was no magic wand anywhere that a modern day Moses waved to part the waters of the Red Sea! You have got to learn to trade the hard way in the crucible called the stock market.

I will let you into a little secret about stock trading. Knowledge though critically important will only take you thus far. What will really take you to the next level has got to be your persistence. All the same, you can never be unprepared. For opportunity, though rare and far between, can present itself any moment and when that happens, you don't want to miss it for anything in the world.

For all you know, that moment might coincide with a very long bull run that might change your fortune overnight. When such an opportunity presents itself, you have got to grab it with both hands and not let someone else walk away with it.

> *"There is a tide in the affairs of men. Which, taken at the flood, leads on to fortune; Omitted, all the voyage of their life is bound in shallows and in miseries. On such a full sea are we now afloat, and we must take the current when it serves, or lose our ventures."*

These immortal lines from Shakespeare's Julius Caesar tell it all. The fact of the matter is that you can make money on the stock of your choosing if you do things right. Not that it will happen overnight or by a miracle. On the contrary, you will have to work very hard for it.

You may have to unlearn your old beliefs and try out new strategies that you are initially not comfortable with. Of course, it is also going to take discipline and the ability to keep on honing and improving one's strategy and not be fazed by temporary setbacks.

That should give you cause to think. The fact of the matter is that you can trade for a living and the question is how. But for that, you should be clear in your head about your reasons for trading.

You have got to have a workable and proven strategy in place and make sure your expectations from trading are realistic. Your trading business plan too has to be in place. The aims and objectives too should be known, probably written down. Now get down to working hard on honing your skills.

The whole concept of making money by speculating on prices of shares of money is the outcome of human ingenuity. In the old days, one either made something or provided a service for which a wage was paid.

This whole business of making untold wealth not by making or selling something, but by speculating about share price may at first seem odd or even immoral. But is it?

Is unleashing and unlocking wealth, which can be put to good use, immoral? By no stretch of the imagination. The reason that I have added a moral dimension to this book is the fact that you should feel good about what you are doing and not ashamed or embarrassed.

I am not assuming you are, but just trying to explain why trading might actually be a noble endeavor, rather than a close relative of gambling. In the times ahead machines, robots and artificial intelligence will have taken away most of our jobs.

There is already talk of a universal basic pension being given to everyone.

So how is trading in any way negative? In the movie Wall Street, Martin Sheen - a factory worker - asks his son, Charlie Sheen a broker, incredulously as he does not make or sell anything, how does he make so much money.

In the movie, Charlie Sheen makes his money the wrong way and pays the penalty for it. So does the character of Charlie's boss Michael Douglas, who famously declares that "greed is good."

Greed is not good, it never is, but trading lawfully is. It is a wealth creator and has the ability to uplift people.

Imagine all those students who can't go for higher education because they can't afford it. Well, trading can certainly help them afford it. People can also pay for their healthcare and possibly contribute handsomely to charity. What is there to not like about trading? Revel in it.

I will let you into a secret. I thoroughly enjoyed

writing this book and as you might well imagine judging by how effusive I have been in parts, I have written it with a lot of passion. This is because I genuinely believe that stock trading has the potential to change the world.

I hope that I have managed to rub off some of my passion on to you. If only a few of the readers are convinced of taking on stock trading as a full time profession on account of reading this book, I will be mighty pleased.

I know the sheer joy that stock trading has brought me and want others to experience it as well. That is why I wanted to share my knowledge with you. Do pass it on to as many people as you can or ask them to buy it. The more people who read it, the better I will feel.

The next step for you is to take all the action steps mentioned above so that the lessons of this book are reinforced and always stay with you. Go ahead and trade and thanks for taking the time to read my words.

Finally, if this book has given you value and helped you in any way, then I'd like to ask you for a favor if you would be kind enough to leave a review for this book on Amazon? It'd be greatly appreciated!

Thank you and good luck!

About the Author

Warren Richmond is a professional trader and investment professional of 10 years.

When he was in college, he got interested in trading and investing early but got frustrated understanding the highly complex topic.

Warren wanted a teaching method that he could easily learn from and develop his trading and investing skills. He soon discovered a teaching series that made him learn faster and better.

Applying the same approach, Warren successfully learned the necessary skills in order to become a professional trader and is now teaching the subject matter through writing books.

With the books that he writes on trading, he hopes to provide great value and help readers interested to learn trading.

www.ingramcontent.com/pod-product-compliance
Lightning Source LLC
Chambersburg PA
CBHW070307230526
45470CB00002B/761